What Smart Sponsors Do

SUPERCHARGE OUR NETWORK MARKETING TEAM

KEITH & TOM "BIG AL" SCHREITER

What Smart Sponsors Do

© 2020 by Keith & Tom "Big Al" Schreiter

Published by Fortune Network Publishing

PO Box 890084

Houston, TX 77289 USA

Telephone: +1 (281) 280-9800

BigAlBooks.com

ISBN-13: 978-1-948197-84-7

CONTENTS

PREFACE

In the beginning.

People are different.

And our new team members are very different from us.

Not everyone joins our business for the same reasons. And since it is their business, it is all about them, not about us.

Too often we are so obsessed with our own goals that we forget that our team members have their own lives and their own goals.

As a smart sponsor, one size does not fit all. We will adjust our leadership approach to fit our new team members' needs.

We can organize our sponsoring duties into these three categories:

> **1. Mentoring.** We will reserve our mentoring time for the elite few who say, "I will do whatever it takes to achieve my goals." These individuals deserve our time and focus. They want step-by-step guidance from us. Here are our future leaders in the making.

> **2. Coaching.** Most of our sponsoring duties will consist of coaching team members on how to build their businesses. Who are these people? They are the team members who promise us, "I will do my best!" That's a great commitment, and we will help them do their best.

3. Psychologist. Some team members have an attitude that makes them think, "I will try. But first, let me look for reasons why this business won't work for me. I will complain and always have reasons that hold me back." For them, we can donate some time to play part-time psychologist. However, we do want to limit our charity work in the beginning of our careers. We need to invest this time in building our business.

This book will concentrate on our mentoring and coaching. We will leave the psychology to the professionals. They have years of training to prepare for this responsibility. We don't.

WE DON'T WANT TO BE THIS PERSON.

Me: "I just started. I am shy. I don't know how to approach and talk to people."

Worthless Sponsor: "Don't waste my time. Bottom line: What is the problem?"

Me: "I am scared of my shadow."

Worthless Sponsor: "Then go out and recruit at night!"

G-r-r-r-r.

We don't want to be this kind of sponsor.

What does the word "sponsor" mean?

Could we agree that it might mean that we should help people who don't know how to navigate through their new career?

It is too easy to see the world from our viewpoint. We forget how incompetent we were when we started. We forget the initial fears that held us back. So yes, it is a challenge to step back and relate to new team members.

But as a smart sponsor, we can step up and have empathy and learn to relate. This isn't that hard to do. We simply start from where **they are** now, and teach them the steps to get where **we are** now.

LAST PLACE? NOT SO BAD.

Early in my career, my sponsor introduced a contest. It was a race to see who could sponsor four new team members first.

I came in … last place.

Which was **ahead** of the people that didn't finish.

And far, **far ahead** of the people that didn't even start.

How did I use my incompetence to beat all those that didn't start, or didn't finish?

Secret #1: Motivation. I wanted to finish.

Yeah, it would have been a lot smarter to learn a skill, but at that time I didn't know about skills. I was full-on incompetence on fire. Motivation was all I had.

How did I get this motivation?

I had to work hard to qualify for last place, really hard. I needed motivation to face the rejection that I caused by using the wrong words. When we don't have skills, we have to work 100 times harder to get the same result. I worked extra hard just to get to last place.

My second secret?

Here is how I got this motivation.

I grew up on a farm. Almost everything we did consisted of big, multi-day projects. How did we manage?

We just started.

Then, continued.

And a few days later, we finished the project and started the next project. My brother and I had a forced habit (Dad woke us up early to start). This is what we did naturally, every day.

Now, from this experience I learned to start work, make progress, and the goal would be achieved automatically. We never thought about the goal. I had never even heard the word "goal" until I started network marketing. All we knew was:

1. To start.

2. Do something we were capable of doing to move us forward.

3. The project would be finished.

What makes the difference?

Look at #2: "Do something we were capable of doing to move us forward."

Notice the words "we were capable of doing." Ah, there is the second secret that holds us back.

In network marketing, we ask people to do things they can't do. They don't know how to perform the task. Ouch!

When this happens, we need to look at what is missing.

1. Are they missing the motivation to attempt the task?

2. Or are they missing the skills to perform the task?

I didn't have a motivation problem when I was young. Dad made sure of that.

And the skills?

Dad always made sure that my brother and I would be doing work that we could perform as kids. Not something scary. Not something impossible. But something we knew how to do.

Most people are not afraid of work. They know building a network marketing business isn't a "free lunch" or something that happens on its own. They are okay with work.

But, they are **not okay** with work they are afraid of, or can't do. What scares them?

- Getting appointments.
- Meeting strangers.
- Giving presentations.
- And for new people, this list goes on and on.

Now we understand why some new, excited team members quit. Their motivation wasn't the problem. They just didn't want to face the rejection and failure that would inevitably arise from their low skill levels.

They thought to themselves, "Hey! I've got enough food in the refrigerator. I don't need this unpleasant feeling of incompetence. Let me relax and watch television instead. Building a business is too hard."

As smart sponsors, we must recognize that new people are not where we are now. This is a brand-new profession for them. We can't expect people to have the skills for every profession in the universe. They didn't learn network marketing skills in school.

KNOW OUR NEW TEAM MEMBER.

Network marketing leader Wes Linden tells a story. He asks one of his alleged great leaders, "And can you tell me the carpet design in your new team member's living room?"

The alleged great leader can't.

How can we communicate and motivate at a deep level if we don't have a good relationship with our new team member? We need to understand:

    1. **Why** they wanted to join the business.

    2. **Where** they want the business to take them.

    3. **How** they want to get there.

Do we know the goals of our personally-sponsored team members? If not, this could be a sign that we need to step up and be better sponsors.

Let's look at these three questions more closely.

#1. Why did our new team members join the business?

My motivation when I started? I didn't want to go to my office job. It was boring, advancement possibilities were years away, and I had no passion for the work I was doing. Keith's motivation? He wanted to earn more money than his high school teachers, so he could concentrate on drumming with his rock band. Two totally different motivations. We need to understand our new team members' motivations.

#2. Where do our new team members want to take their business?

For some team members, a part-time income to pay off credit card debt might be the only goal. They enjoy their current professions. Or they don't feel that their lives are secure unless they have salaried jobs. Other new team members might want to earn enough money to buy a small country. We will have different conversations with each of these team members.

#3. How do our new team members want to get to their business goals?

John wishes to keep his reputation with his accounting friends. He only wants to promote his business to people he doesn't know. Mary, on the other hand, can't wait to tell everyone she knows about the business.

Some people want to take the slow route, while others will throw caution to the wind and do whatever it takes to get there immediately.

Talking to people directly is comfortable for some team members. Others are more cautious and want to spend more time building a relationship or educating their prospects.

Team members are individuals. One system or strategy isn't perfect for everyone. Jessica loves to entertain. When we mention an in-home launch party, Jessica is already preparing the refreshments and writing out the invitation list. This is her comfort zone. She entertains regularly and can't wait to expand her business this way.

Another team member has no local contacts. An in-home launch party makes no sense. No one would come. With phone contacts spread throughout the country, we must use a different approach. We'll need to ask ourselves, "How does this new team member want to communicate? What will feel more natural?"

Here are some of the many ways that new team members can contact people:

- Phone call
- Social media
- Texting
- In-person meeting
- Email
- In-home launch party
- Zoom call

These three questions give us the big picture. It is hard to design successful paths for our new team members without these guidelines.

EXAMPLES OF THESE QUESTIONS IN ACTION.

Bob's story.

One of my first leaders was Bob. As a systems analyst and an ultra-green personality, he was not naturally outgoing. Here is how he answered these three questions.

#1. Why do I want this business? Bob answered, "I commute two hours daily on the train. My job pays well, but I work with other boring programmers who have no goals. We never talk about what else we could do with our lives. I want to have my own business, to be an investor, and spend more time with my six children. I believe I can earn more if I actually get paid what I am worth."

As a fellow green personality, it was easy for me to build a connection with Bob. We saw the world from the same viewpoint. Engineers, accountants, and computer programmers understand leverage and compounding our efforts. We instantly see the power of network marketing.

Unfortunately, as green personalities, our people skills are usually lacking. It takes more than math skills to build a business. No one ever joins network marketing because of a calculation. We have to deal with people. The good news? We can learn these skills!

#2. Where do I want to take this business? Bob answered, "I want a full-time income. With travel time, my job takes up to 11 hours out of my day. I can do more than oversee other programmers. Managing people and filling out forms will only take me so far. With a full-time income, I can spend time studying and making investments for a secure future."

Bob had a plan. He wanted to invest in real estate and stocks, and get his cash flow from a full-time network marketing business. He educated himself on different investments, our company's product line, and how to be a more effective networker.

Did Bob's plan work out? No.

Going outside of his comfort zone and making new networking contacts didn't fit his personality. He took a more passive approach. His business grew slowly and never progressed beyond a good part-time income. But he used his part-time income to pay off his house. Then used his part-time income plus the money that would normally go towards the mortgage to invest. Eventually he arrived at his goal, a full-time income from network marketing and investments, mostly from his investments.

#3. How do I want to get to my business goal? Bob didn't make cold calls. He didn't join networking groups. Instead, he let the product benefits gradually build a base of loyal users. This took longer, but it was within Bob's comfort zone. He enjoyed sharing product benefits. I supported Bob's plan to consistently build in a way that he enjoyed.

Sylvia's story.

Another one of my early leaders was Sylvia. She was a beautician with her own small beauty shop. No employees, only Sylvia. Here is how she answered these three questions.

#1. Why do I want this business? Sylvia answered, "I am 48 years old. I stand on my feet for nine hours a day helping my customers look beautiful. I do this six days a week, with only Mondays off. Then I rush out and buy more beauty supplies for the week. At the end of the day I am too tired to have a social life. I can't see myself doing this for the next 17 years until I retire."

Sylvia didn't understand the compensation plan. She had no idea how rank advancements worked. But she was a natural networker, talking to people every day. She knew how to listen and talk to people about their interests.

#2. Where do I want to take this business? Sylvia answered, "I want to qualify for the car. I've never had a new car in my life, and now is the time to do it. Especially if someone else pays for it. And I can qualify for trips? That sounds exciting. I know where my current career will take me, and I don't want to go there. If all I have to do is talk to people to have a new career, I can do that. I want to leave my beauty shop behind."

Sometimes building leaders is easy. Not only do they have internal motivation, but they already have great networking and communication skills. Sylvia knew where she wanted to go. She was not going to get distracted by shiny objects or time-wasting activities.

#3. How do I want to get to my business goal? For Sylvia, this was easy. She had a captive audience of regular customers. These customers knew her, liked her, and trusted her. There was no need to build additional rapport. All she had to do was use a good ice breaker, and the customers made an instant decision. Plus, Sylvia had walk-in traffic to her shop. Every week she met new prospects. She didn't have to make cold calls, join a net-working group, or do anything outside of her comfort zone. All she had to do was learn how to more effectively talk to her current prospects.

Sylvia qualified for her car. She won her first trip. She doubled her previous beautician income, closed the shop, and never looked back. She had a clear goal, and she built her entire business within her comfort zone.

Mr. Poh's story.

In the early 1990s, China began to open up for network marketing. My friend, Mr. Poh, decided entrepreneurship made sense. Here is how he answered these three questions.

#1. Why do I want this business? Mr. Poh answered, "The future is China, but not quite yet. It will take time to change decades of rigid thinking. I can help my family and friends dream about new possibilities. Being an entrepreneur and owning a business will be difficult. But I want to be part of the change. When no one believes, I want to be the one shining light in their memories that believed in them and their future. I want respect."

Sometimes we forget that our careers are more than money. Our careers can give hope to others and change their lives. Think about the many motivations humans have. Recognition, power, a sense of contribution, leaving a legacy, the ability to change lives, and a chance to inspire people to do more than they thought they could. The satisfaction from a network marketing career could be more important than a bonus check. We will spend the money, but the memories and fulfillment of helping others through network marketing will last forever.

#2. Where do I want to take this business? Mr. Poh answered, "I see myself speaking to skeptical groups. As a sales leader, people will come out of respect for my message. It is what I will teach at these group meetings that will multiply my influence on others. I want to go from city to city to introduce people to the power of network marketing. They won't get a guarantee, but they will have an opportunity to change their lives."

Mr. Poh had a yellow personality. He only saw this business through the lens of how he could help others.

#3. How do I want to get to my business goal? For Mr. Poh, this was easy. He wanted to speak three times a day training people in a new way of thinking called, "network marketing." He loved to teach. He loved standing in front of a room. This was so enjoyable for him that he would have done it for free. He went from city to city, promoted his business, asked people to come to his trainings, and built the business of his dreams. All I had to do was provide him with the basic concept of network marketing and then stay out of his way.

Why these three basic questions?

These are the foundations of how we can motivate, guide, and train our new team members. Let's look at these questions one by one, and see what they can help us accomplish.

#1. WHY DO I WANT THIS BUSINESS?

If our new team members join our business on a whim, it won't take much of a breeze to topple their business. There will be rough times ahead. No business is a straight line to success with zero obstacles.

Once we know the "why," we can regularly remind new team members of their internal motivation. Here's an example.

John's "why" is to retire his spouse from her job. We have a phone conversation with John where he tells us that he sponsored a new distributor. We can reply, "That is great. You will be helping another person achieve their dreams. Plus, that is one step closer to retiring your spouse from her job. I know she will be so happy."

Sometimes when we are feeling down, we forget the "why" of our mission. It is easier to keep our team members' internal motivation strong when we remind them of their "why."

It is better to remind John of his "why" when things are good. It comes across as blackmail if we bring up the "why" when things are bad. We may not say this, but John might interpret whatever we say as, "So you want to quit? I guess that means you don't care about helping your spouse retire." Yeah, that is pretty cold.

What about bonding? When we talk to others about their deepest desires and goals, we form strong bonds that last through challenges. Many describe network marketing as a relationship business.

This is not like transactions on the Internet. It is not a one-time exchange of money for services. This explains why some groups stay together and are loyal, while other groups quickly disintegrate and look for the next hot deal.

Here is the motivation principle we should remember:

"Most people are moving away from their problems, not moving towards their goals."

Our new team members join. We think, "Wow. They want what I have to offer."

But that might not be the reality.

More likely, their initial motivation is to avoid the pain of their current situations. Think about these examples.

Example #1. Do people randomly show up at a car dealership and decide to buy a car? No. They are moving away from their problem. What problem? The current car is old and breaking down. Or, their friends have better cars and they want to be like their friends.

Example #2. The sink in our kitchen is broken. Why do we go to the local DIY store? Because we want to move away from our problem.

When we have problems, we tell ourselves, "Let's go look for a way to get rid of this problem. What possible solutions are out there?"

So when new team members join our business, we can assume they are moving away from their problems. They are moving away from poverty, lack of time, or feeling crushed with no freedom options. Or, they might be moving away from an unfulfilled life, and can't wait to share our products and services with others.

They may not admit their problems to us, but their problems motivated them to look for change.

People will do more to eliminate a problem then they will to work for a goal. People hate problems.

#2. WHERE DO I WANT TO TAKE THIS BUSINESS?

Early in my career, I made the mistake of thinking everyone wanted to fire their bosses and have their own full-time business. I was wrong. That is how I viewed the business. It definitely was not how most of my team members viewed the business.

Some wanted a little extra spending money. I remember a man from Missouri who told me, "I earned $50 last month in the business." This didn't seem like much, yet he was excited. I wondered why.

He continued, "I don't earn much in my job. After paying the expenses for our family, I am left with $5 a month of spending money to call my own. With this extra $50, I have ten times more spending money than I've ever had before. I can go to a store and buy something. I can have a meal at a restaurant. This is life-changing for me."

For him, a small part-time income was his immediate focus. He didn't think bigger than $50 a month yet. It would be a disservice for me to insist he look at the big picture and change his mind. Instead, I should help him repeat his monthly income at this level until he is ready to want more for his life.

For other team members? They could want to build a large part-time income to finance their favorite charity. The larger the part-time income, the more people the charity could help. For these team members, I would remind them what others have done for their charity of choice. This helps them keep their focus and continue working even during busy times in their lives. They know that consistent effort to build residual income is necessary for their charity's budget.

I sponsored Mike. He wanted to take his business to a full-time income in one week. We had a problem.

Mike learned every shortcut and magic tip he could. No relationships, no community, no long-term strategy. This was a bad match. It finally ended with Mike leaving the business for a get-rich scheme. It was good to recognize early that Mike's unrealistic goals would sabotage his work. This saved us both future grief.

"Where do I want to take this business?" This question helps us chart a better path with our team members.

What if team members find it difficult to set goals?

Here are two quick solutions for that problem.

New team members may be shy and reluctant to state their goals. They won't write anything down. So as smart sponsors, we need to get rid of their inhibitions. How?

1. In our leadership books, we talked about this method. We asked the team member to write down 25 things they are going to do AFTER they reach a certain goal. This might seem intimidating to new team members, so let's say this: "Please write down three things you are going to do after you get your first big bonus check."

2. Here is another method that is even shorter. Network marketing pro Lloyd Daley from England says, "Let's

pretend ..." Pretending doesn't sound so intimidating to new team members. They can pretend that a certain achievement could be met, and that becomes a goal.

This takes the pressure off new team members and allows them to dream.

The next question, question #3, is huge. Let's spend the next chapter learning its secrets.

#3. HOW DO I WANT TO GET TO MY BUSINESS GOAL?

Think of a goal as a direction we want to go.

But directions don't make things happen.

It is the activity we do that moves us towards our goals that counts. Too many new team members will set goals and think their job is done. The reality? Setting the goal means we know the direction we want to go, but we are not there.

"How do I want to get to my business goal?" The startling fact is that we must customize the answer to fit the current talents of our new team members.

This is huge. Here is why:

1. We recognize that each of our new team members has individual talents and resources.

2. We know new team members have internal programs that prevent them from utilizing certain methods of building their business.

It is too easy to believe our way is the only way. Our experiences prove to us that what we believe is true. And once we find this ultimate "truth," we want to preach our truth to everyone. Egotistical leaders do this often. An example of this "truth" going wrong?

The leader drives home from a motivational rally. He is too excited to pay attention to his driving. What happens? The leader hits the car in front of him. The other driver gets out, holding his neck, and the leader immediately says, "Here! Take these magic vitamins." The next day, the other driver calls the leader and says, "Wow! I feel great from these vitamins. My neck is okay, and I have more energy than a hyperactive squirrel on caffeine. How do I join?"

What happens? The leader sponsors his very best distributor ever. The leader thinks he has discovered the system to success. What's next? Teaching this secret magic system of success to the team. He instructs the team to rear-end cars while driving. From his experience, this is the best way to get the best new leaders.

It gets brutal. If team members refuse to cause car accidents, they aren't loyal. "Get off the team! And don't bother sponsoring people who can't drive. Those losers can never do the business."

Do we see the problem? What worked for the leader may not work for everyone on the team. Everyone has different assets, skills, and abilities. Here are some examples.

One leader has 96 first cousins. His advice? "Only talk to your relatives. That is what worked best for me." And if we don't have enough relatives, he instructs us to get married a few times so that we have more in-laws to talk to.

Another leader instructs his group to call 25 strangers every day. This may work for the leader who has thick skin and great telephone skills. But, this will be hard for others to duplicate without his natural abilities.

Insisting on duplication only works if everyone has the same background, skills and circumstances. That seldom happens.

So what should we duplicate?

We want to duplicate the result.

We don't have to duplicate the same strategy for retailing and sponsoring. We should encourage new team members to build in ways that feel comfortable for them.

If the day-to-day activities of prospecting, retailing, and sponsoring are uncomfortable, our team members will stop.

Think of it this way. Imagine we get paid money to hit our hand with a hammer. Yes, we enjoy the money, but at some point we will stop. When the pain gets bad enough, no matter what the reward, we will want to stop.

Network marketing is a long-term career. We want team members to enjoy it.

How to make the day-to-day activities of our team members enjoyable.

Let's find out how new team members prefer to talk to people. If we can incorporate business-building activities into their daily routines, then our team members will be much more comfortable.

Shoppers. If our new team member loves shopping, what a great, natural way to meet new people. We can provide a perfect ice breaker for sales clerks, people standing in line, and even for the cashiers. Then, our new team member can simply take the volunteers. Now this is a reason to shop even more!

Here is an example. In conversation with sales clerks, they could say, "I am curious, could you do me a favor? I am looking for people who want a change of career where they can set their own hours for work. Do you know anyone like that?"

The sales clerks could politely say they don't know anyone, or express their personal interest immediately. No rejection. This is easy to do, and it only took seconds.

This works for products and services also. The team member could say, "I am curious, could you do me a favor? I am looking for grandparents who want a way to have more energy than their grandchildren. Do you know anyone like that?"

Golfers. When a team member is stuck with three other people on the golf course for three hours, he doesn't have to rely only on a quick ice breaker. He has plenty of time to build rapport. Our team member loves golfing regularly, and will enjoy his daily prospecting activity.

Stay-at-home parents. What about social media, video calls, and social time chatting with other parents while watching children play in the park? Sound like a plan?

We can do many more examples. The point is that **we must make the process enjoyable.**

If you've read the book *3 Easy Habits for Network Marketing*, then you know that habit #2 is entirely about getting people to talk to one new person a day. And they do this in a way that is within that person's comfort zone.

Comfort zones are important. It is when we feel uncomfortable that we look for reasons to procrastinate or quit.

"Recent studies show that avoiding prospects increases business failures over 100%."

Okay, slightly exaggerated. But we get the point. Building a network marketing business requires us to locate and talk to new prospects. This is what we do. We can't get decisions if we are not talking to anyone.

If our new team members have a constant supply of new prospects, their stress levels go down. They won't worry about their eventual success. They know it will be inevitable. If they have a bad week and no one is interested, they know that next week can be better.

Having new, fresh prospects to talk to cures most problems.

We need to set them up with a daily routine that guarantees their eventual success.

Yes, this could be a different routine for each new member. However, it is worthwhile to spend the time to make this happen. Once the routine is in place, we've set the foundation for their success.

As our group grows, our bonus check will represent less of what we do, but will reflect more of what our group does.

We create an environment for our individual team members where they can enjoy their work, feel respected, and be recognized for their efforts.

Make it impossible to quit.

Nobody quits network marketing when they have prospects and appointments lined up.

We don't know if the next prospect is going to be the one person that makes us rich. And if our current prospect is undecided, we don't panic. We have more prospects waiting.

How do our team members get all these prospects and appointments? Well, it is different for everyone. Some people just use a social media strategy. Other people use the bird dog strategy. And others, maybe they use the "Stair Step Solution," or have another great way to get new referrals.

We are all different. We enjoy different methods of prospecting. What is important is that we find the methods our new team members enjoy. I like to ask this question:

"What would be the most comfortable way for you to find new prospects?"

Then, listen.

Then listen some more.

Our new distributor will tell us what they like. Some like to call people, some like in-person prospecting. Others want to run ads. Some have special marketing skills that they want to use. It doesn't matter how they want to prospect; what matters is that they find a way that works for them.

Are these the only questions we can ask our new team members?

No.

If we have empathy, we know the direction our conversations and trainings should go. For example, let's imagine that our new team members don't seem 100% committed to their goals. We could ask a few more questions to help them reaffirm their commitment.

MORE QUESTIONS, MORE STORIES.

The first three questions give us the basic information we need to be great sponsors.

Are there other questions we could ask? Yes. But it depends on the situation. We will notice that some people might be afraid of selling. Others don't know where to start. Some may have issues with limited time.

Let's look at a few optional questions that could help us get our new team members started faster.

"What kinds of problems do you think we will encounter?"

Yes, there will always be problems. We want to talk about these problems before they happen. They are much easier to deal with beforehand.

Our team members begin to think. "What are some of the bad things that could happen to us?" We want them to come up with a list. Their list might look something like this:

- No one wants to talk to me.
- My family tells me "no" and then I don't want to continue.
- My friends won't believe me.
- Everyone I know is lazy.

- I will find out that I don't like selling.

- My closest friends tell me to quit.

- I work hard for three months and then lose money.

- Four people in a row hang up on me. For me, that would be a sign to quit.

- My spouse will tell me not to do this.

- No one wants to buy. They think it is too expensive.

- I don't earn enough money for my time.

- It takes up too much time and my family complains.

- They might ask me, "So how much money will it cost me to join?"

Now is the time to talk about these problems.

Here is an example of why we do this. We sponsor a new team member. The new team member talks to his best friend, who joins but quits the next day. This feels devastating to the person we sponsored. The event has already happened. We are in recovery mode. This is hard.

But what if we talked about this type of event happening beforehand? Maybe our new team member said, "If my best friend joins and then quits, that won't be enough to drive me out of this business. I can still be successful without my best friend on my team."

Then, when this event happens, he is mentally prepared. Prevention is better than being in crisis recovery mode.

When we ask about the kinds of problems that our new team members are worried about, we also reap another benefit. We help our new team members mature and accept that problems are part of growing our business. Problems happen all the time. This business is no exception.

Will our new team members quit because of a problem and go to our competition? No. Don't worry. Our competition has problems too. If someone wants to prevent problems, changing companies won't solve the problem. When new team members realize this, they will be able to withstand the first few problems in their careers.

COMMON BUMPS IN THE ROAD.

When we sponsor enough people, we start to notice a pattern. The same objections and stumbling blocks occur over and over.

We have many tools in our sponsor toolbox that will help us create guidelines for our new people.

One of our most effective tools? Stories.

Stories are the best way for our minds to learn. Think about it. Fairytales are pretty grim. But they teach children lessons about fearing strangers, being too greedy, etc.

Our minds are designed to look for meaning inside of stories, and this helps us remember them.

Let's apply the story technique to our first stumbling block.

"Someone told me they were not interested."

We love the enthusiasm of new team members. They quickly saw the opportunity, and assumed that everyone else would see the great opportunity also.

Well, as we know, it doesn't usually happen that way.

In the first few days, rejection can shake their confidence. Close friends tell them, "This is not for me. I don't do these kinds of things."

Our new team members think, "What? Did I make a mistake? Let me rethink my commitment here."

An easy way to calm our new team members is with a story. Stories are great ways to get our lessons across.

The lottery ticket.

You have lottery tickets for sale. Everyone wants a lottery ticket because tomorrow is the big drawing. Tomorrow is the jackpot of all jackpots. There is a single-file line of 1,000 people waiting to buy from you.

The first person says, "I will buy a lottery ticket from you. I want my chance at the big drawing tomorrow."

The second person says, "Yes, I want to buy a lottery ticket. I can't win or even have a chance of winning unless I have a ticket."

The third person says, "I am not sure. I may not win the lottery. Let me research the history of the lottery first. I need to talk to my friends. What will happen if it doesn't work out for me? This could be a government lottery scam. Why can't you guarantee that I will win? I want you to talk to me and convince me. Please spend the next two weeks following up with me and invest your valuable time into getting me to change my mind."

The 997 people waiting in line are getting impatient. Plus, you want to sell your lottery tickets in time to go home and have dinner with your family.

We ask our new team member, "What would you do in this situation?"

Our new team member replies, "I would agree with the skeptical third person. I would tell him that he is correct, and he should go home and think about it. Then when I am rich and famous, I could donate my time to help him change his attitude in life. But for now, I need to sell these lottery tickets and build my career."

Our new team member now understands that not everybody in the line will be ready to buy lottery tickets. That is okay. We don't take it personally. We don't have to worry about their reasons for not buying.

For example, someone in line might say, "I will not buy a lottery ticket. I refuse to buy anything that starts with the letter 'L'!" And for us, that is okay. If our lottery tickets are not good options for some of the people in line, then those people should do what is right for their lives.

This is a great guide on how we should approach retailing and sponsoring.

We want people who want what we offer. If our offer is a good option for them, they should take advantage of it. If our offer is not a good option for them, we should go to the next person.

Now, this is easy for us to see, but what might happen inside our new members' minds?

They might think, "I only have a few friends. I don't have 1,000 people in line waiting to talk to me. My prospects are limited. If someone tells me they are not interested, I must convince them because I have no one else to talk to."

This is why we teach new people Habit #2. We teach them ways to prospect every day within their comfort zones. These ways must be comfortable and rejection-free for them.

When they visualize a steady stream of new prospects in the future, it will be easier for them to embrace the lottery story. They won't waste time trying to convince a skeptic. And they won't have to worry about rejection.

Stories are fun. But we have more tools that we can use to help out our new team members.

How about analogies? Let's take a look.

THE POWER OF ANALOGIES.

Analogies and metaphors help new team members understand the principles in our business. Humans can find it difficult to understand new things, unless they can compare the new information to something they already know. Here is an example.

We see a picture of a cup. No background. How big is the cup? Is it the size of a car? Is it the size of a pencil eraser? We don't know. The only way we can guess the size of the cup is to place another familiar object in the picture. In this case, we put a human hand near the cup. Now our minds can understand the size of the cup.

Here is what's interesting. If someone tells us a fact, such as the size of the cup, we will forget it. If we come to our own conclusion about the size of the cup, it is easier for us to remember. Our brains remember our conclusions.

Let's put this to work.

Our new team member has a job. He gets the same paycheck every week. Some weeks he works hard, and some weeks he doesn't, but his check remains the same. He has a salary.

This is not how network marketing works. With network marketing, you will only get paid for your personal production. No sales, no money. Lots of sales, lots of money.

The only thing that counts is if our new team members can get some "yes" decisions from prospects. How can we communicate this with an analogy or story? Here is how.

The patio painting story.

You hire me to paint your patio. You say, "I'm leaving today for my one-week holiday. While I am away, paint my patio. My patio is small, so it should only take you a day to finish. When I return in one week, I will pay you."

Since no one works on weekends, this leaves me with five working days to paint your house. Let's log my activity for those five days:

> Day 1: Celebrate my new painting contract at the local bar with my friends. Drinks for everyone!
>
> Day 2: Recover from a vicious hangover.
>
> Day 3: Study the history of paint.
>
> Day 4: Decide what I am going to do with the money I will get from you.
>
> Day 5: Visualize what a painted patio would look like.

You return from your holiday. I say to you, "Please pay me for my work."

When you look at your patio, you see no results. Not a single drop of paint can be seen anywhere.

Will you pay me? No. You tell me, "You have no results. Nothing was accomplished. I only pay for results."

So does it matter that I worked five full days on your painting project? No. My activity produced zero results. If I repeated the same schedule the following week, I still wouldn't have any results.

And that is how network marketing works. We get paid for results. We don't get paid for effort. We don't get paid for thinking about it. We don't get paid for time invested. The only thing we get paid for is getting "yes" decisions.

Learning, taking notes, creating vision boards, attending motivational rallies, and visiting with prospects won't count towards our bonus checks. What counts is results.

Of course we should learn. We should have dreams and goals. We want to be mentally strong. However, we don't want to confuse these with income-producing activities that yield results. At some point, we actually have to go out and do the work.

Ready for another analogy?

Our new team member says, "I am afraid to get started. I am afraid of what other people might say. I don't think I can cope with rejection. I am not a salesperson. Pestering my friends to buy or join would leave a bad taste in my mouth. I don't think I can deal with all of this fear."

How should we respond? Of course we could be silly and say things such as:

- "Face the fear, and the fear will go away."
- "The only way to conquer fear is to work through it."
- "Reclaim your power by refusing to feel fear."

Human brains don't work like this. We avoid scary situations.

How can we give our new team member a way to deal with this fear? With an analogy. We will say this:

"Fear is good. Fear prevents us from doing stupid stuff. We won't let it prevent us from reaching our goals, but it is a necessary emotion we must have to survive.

"Imagine you want to go to the store to buy food for the family. Driving is dangerous. Our fear prevents us from taking unnecessary risks along the way. Thank goodness we have fear so that we can come back alive with food for the family.

"It is the same in network marketing. Our fear should prevent us from saying and doing stupid things. Our fear should prevent us from continuing conversations with people that are uninterested. Our fear will teach us to get to the point immediately so that we don't irritate prospects. And finally, our fear will help us have empathy with our prospects. Now we can see things from their points of view and present to them exactly what they want.

"You have fear? Great! Keep the fear. It is there to keep you safe and to remind you to have good manners when talking to others. We are here to serve others, not to sell them something they don't want or need."

How about another analogy?

New team members can create a lot of drama inside their heads. They will imagine rejection, struggles, and frustration ... before anything even happens! Here is our chance to reduce this fear so that our new team members can be more productive.

Now is a good time to change their viewpoint from prospecting and selling to sharing an option.

Here is our story.

"Selling implies that we must convince prospects to buy against their will. This doesn't feel right. It is like approaching someone with a milk allergy and trying to sell that person ice cream. No matter how powerful our closing techniques, we will not succeed.

"Instead, look at our new network marketing business this way. We have millions of prospects who want what we have to offer. We offer them an option to buy our products or services or join our business. They can take our option if now is a good time for them.

"What about the people who are not interested in what we have to offer? There is no need for us to disagree or try to convert them. Not everyone likes chocolate, a particular sports team, or our products. This is why we have variety in the world. Allow prospects to choose what is best for them. But please, don't keep our option a secret from them."

Think of the internal peace this brings to new team members. They won't take rejection personally. They still want to offer options to new people. And they won't question their network marketing business because some people said, "No."

If they feel frustrated because they are not getting results, we will remind them that with better skills and experience, their options will get more takers.

"Options" is a powerful word. It relieves our stress and our prospects' stress. Here is Keith's favorite "options" story:

"Imagine you and I are sitting down with a cup of coffee. The waitress approaches and says, 'Would you like cream with your coffee?' And you reply, 'Yes.'

"Next the waitress asks me, 'Would you like cream with your coffee?' And I reply, 'No. I prefer my coffee black.'

"We don't see the waitress go back into the kitchen, slam her cream against the wall and scream, 'I have been rejected! I quit! This is a pyramid!'

"No. Cream was just an option. The waitress shouldn't be concerned that you wanted cream while I did not."

Using analogies makes it easier for people to understand new concepts. With good stories and analogies, new team members will learn fast.

THE POWER OF ANALOGIES.

Two important mindset principles:

#1. People hate presentations. Presentations mean we will try to sell them something. They have to look for reasons why it won't work, so they have ammunition in case we try to close them at the end.

Instead, we will use the "options" word. Options mean it is okay to say "yes" or "no." But the only way for options to benefit our prospects is if they can figure out a way for the options to work for them. That means they will be looking for reasons why, and not reasons why not. Now prospects relax and listen with open minds.

#2. Network marketing is something that we do **for** someone, not **to** someone. People pick up on our intention by looking at our body language, micro-facial expressions, and tone of voice. All these things happen in the first few seconds.

Instead of looking for "prospects," we will want our team members to replace "prospects" with "people I can help." Now we won't hear phrases such as, "I am going out to look for prospects." Instead, they will change their mindsets to, "I am going out to look for people that I can help."

HOW TO GET MASSIVE ACTION WITHIN OUR TEAM.

Leading up to the company convention, the team works hard. They talk to new people. They set appointments. And they double their activities to qualify for convention recognition.

And after the exciting convention? Nothing. The team waits for another sale, promotion, or big event. Things get quiet. Momentum comes to a halt. And then it gets worse. Team members complain that the business is not working. They don't earn the money they believe they deserve. No one wants to join.

As sponsors, we see these cycles over and over again. It's draining. It's frustrating. And we want to fix it.

But how do we get consistent action from our part-time team members who have other priorities in their lives? This business might be our life, but not theirs.

To fix this, we have to understand human nature.

Humans like communities. Humans like to be part of something. Very few of us want to be loners and social outcasts. We will use this knowledge to start building consistent activity and volume for our team.

The plan.

Let's look at our current part-time members' lives. Our team members:

- Think about our business between television shows.

- Set goals and forget them.

- Have too many distractions.

- Have no simple strategy.

This obviously won't work. But before we proceed, what do we want to accomplish? We want our team members to:

- Think about our business every week.

- Prospect regularly.

- Bond and become more loyal.

- Love the social connections.

- Feel active and involved.

- Build a belief in their business.

- Develop more skills.

Too good to be true? Let's see how we will accomplish this.

The weekly video conference report.

Organize a once-a-week online team meeting. The online team meeting will be only 20 or 30 minutes at the most. Why?

1. We want to conserve our time.

2. Our teams will love the online team meetings and will attend if they are short. They will look forward to them.

What will we accomplish during our team meeting?

We want to give our team members an easy assignment that will build their business. As we know, lessons and notes are good for memorizing skills. But results come when we put the skills into **action.**

This weekly meeting is not for instruction and taking notes. This weekly meeting is for … action!

No action = no results.

So what would this easy assignment be?

To say one simple sentence, once a day.

This sentence will be an ice breaker sentence that gives prospects choices. When prospects reply to this sentence, they make a choice. That makes closing automatic.

We must make sure that this sentence is rejection-free, and that there is no chance of embarrassment. We want our team members to easily say this sentence once a day. Here are some examples:

- For utilities: "Does it make sense to lower our bills, instead of keeping them high?" Or, "Would it be okay if your electricity bill was lower?"

- For dieting: "Would it be okay if we could lose weight just by changing what we have for breakfast?" Or, "I just found out how we can turn our bodies into fat-burning machines."

- For skincare: "Would it be okay if we could fix our wrinkles from the inside?" Or, "I just found out how we can make our skin younger while we sleep."

- For our opportunity: "Does it make sense to get paid two times a month, instead of only one time a month?" Or, "Would it be okay if we could work from home, instead of commuting to our jobs?"

- For travel: "If you want to pay wholesale instead of retail prices when you travel, let's talk." Or, "Does it make sense to get paid every time our friends go on vacation?"

These are just a few examples of basic ice breakers that compel people to make an instant decision. And did we notice that all of these sentences were safe?

Every team member will pick a sentence they would like to say. Make sure they pick something comfortable so they will be happy and relaxed when talking to prospects.

Let's plan our 20-minute Zoom team meeting.

First, welcome everyone.

Next, we give our personal report first. Why? Not to impress the team members, but to help everyone relax. No one ever wants to go first.

Our report will sound something like this.

"I chose this as my sentence this week: 'If working out of your home sounds better than commuting to work, let's talk.' I said this sentence six times this week. My results? Three people wanted to have a conversation immediately. And here is another great thing that happened to me this week. My son came home with his first passing grade in math. His tutor is doing a great job."

That is it. Our report might take 30 seconds. Our personal report will have these four things:

1. The sentence we chose.

2. How many times we said our sentence.

3. Our results from saying our sentence.

4. And something good that happened to us this week.

Here is why we do these four things.

#1. By repeating our sentence, it helps us improve. Plus, some team members on the call might want to use our sentence next week. Maybe it feels better for them than their current sentence.

#2. When we tell everyone how many times we said our sentence, that is our accountability report. This is ... action! Our job is only to say the sentence. We can't control the lives of the prospects who hear our sentence. This helps motivate us to say the sentence often. We don't want to report that we only said the sentence one time over the entire week. That would be embarrassing.

#3. We report our results from saying our sentence. Remember, we are not attached to the results. But reporting our results lets others know that some people will be interested and some won't, and that is normal.

#4. Report something good that happened to us this week. Nobody wants to hear our negativity and problems. They can hear negativity on the news after we finish. Instead, if everyone reports one good thing that happened, it gives the listeners social proof that good things can happen in our lives. When we hear all these good things happening, we build a belief that no matter how bad this week was for us, next week could be better.

Well, we volunteered to go first. Our turn is finished. Now it is the next person's turn.

Everyone takes their turn and reports. For some, this will help them overcome their shyness. They are with a group of supporters, and this may be the first time they've spoken in public or to a group. It is great personal development.

After each team member finishes, we should compliment the team member for participating in reporting. We make no judgment if team members don't say their sentence at all, or if they couldn't remember how to report these four things. We encourage everyone.

After the reports from everyone, we will give a word or two of motivation. After all, we are the leader of this meeting. We could say something like this:

- "I absolutely know you will all get to Super Executive Director. We don't know how fast, but everyone gets closer every week."

- "You don't know what will happen next week. One person you speak with might earn you $20,000. They just have to hear your sentence."

- "Our job is to give people a chance to have the life of their dreams. Say your chosen sentence. Our obligation is to give others a chance. The rest is up to them."

Next?

This weekly team meeting is also a study group. We will choose one book to study. (Biased viewpoint coming ... Big Al books are great for this.) Don't make this hard. Pick an easy book. And then assign one chapter a week. We want short chapters when we start. Building a habit takes time.

We can have a group discussion for a few minutes of our biggest takeaways and insights from the chapter. Maybe we can share what we are going to put into action this week.

This means everyone attending is getting better every week.

And finally, we can make any announcements.

That is it.

Our weekly call is over.

For our team members, this is a chance to catch up and see what their friends are doing every week. They will look forward to the meeting. And at the end of every call, everyone wants to do better the following week.

Use this simple 20-minutes-a-week investment to put life back into our business. This is one way to get everyone on the team active and involved.

As sponsors, we should already have a library of great first sentences. If not, here are two of our books to start: *Ice Breakers* and *First Sentences for Network Marketing*. This will give us hundreds of sentence possibilities.

If you find that your group is enthusiastic about this short weekly team event, most of them will want their own book for their weekly reading. This is personal development at work.

But, be creative. Keith has one group that has been studying *Think and Grow Rich* every week for 20+ years.

This is like a class reunion every week. :) And as a bonus, if we associate with serious people who want to learn together, it rubs off.

Associating with negative people? That rubs off, too. This is better.

That is why this weekly action meeting works.

A GREAT WAY TO EXPLAIN HOW TO START.

I enjoy listening to how other people explain network marketing. Some years ago, I picked up this gem while listening to Pete Hamby. He explained how he starts new team members by saying:

There are two types of network marketers.

1. Those that "know who" and …

2. Those that "know how."

In the beginning, new team members know prospects. They are the "know who."

New team members have a warm, fresh market of family, friends, and acquaintances. They won't have to worry about building rapport with cold prospects. They already have an audience.

But do new team members know what to say? Do they know how our business works? Of course not. There is a knowledge gap. They don't know how to explain their business. Their approaches and presentations could turn people off.

As sponsors, we are the "know how." New team members can connect us to their initial prospects. While we explain how our business works to their new prospects, they can observe and learn.

Eventually, our new team members will graduate from "know who" to "know how."

Then, they can help their new team members in the same way we helped them.

Keith and I like helping new team members. It takes the pressure off them. They feel safe while observing. And if the prospect is a jerk, the new team members can sit back and observe the carnage. No harm done to the new team members' egos.

This is a win-win-win for everyone.

The new team member won't be nervous trying to give his or her first presentation. The sponsor will be busy giving presentations and building the team.

And the prospects? They get professional presentations, and can make a better decision if our business is for them or not.

But what if new team members are afraid to contact prospects?

The new team members complain, "I am afraid to sell. I am not a salesperson, outgoing, or pushy. I don't want to sell."

That is pretty clear feedback from our new team members. How can we deal with this? Here are some strategies.

Strategy #1. Explain that fear is a basic, automatic emotion. We can't choose not to be fearful and cautious. This is a good emotion for humans to have. Fear keeps us from doing dumb things and helps us survive.

If we fear talking to others, our fear will help us construct a better approach, a better first sentence, and a more empathetic presentation. We will take extra efforts to be polite. These are good things.

Strategy #2. Bad feelings? These are self-induced.

The bigger question is, "Why do we feel bad?"

This comes from when we try to "sell" prospects something they do not need. We have a twisted view that selling is getting people to do something that will not help them. We've probably seen too many old movies of sleazy used-car salesmen trying to manipulate people to buy overpriced cars.

Instead, let's adjust our view of the sales process.

Here is how selling works.

> Step 1. Listen to our prospects to see if they have a problem.
>
> Step 2. Ask our prospects if they want to fix their problem.
>
> Step 3. Find out when our prospects want to fix their problem - now, or sometime in the future.
>
> Step 4. If they want to fix their problems now, we give them the option of what we offer, or they can continue keeping their lives the same.

This view of selling removes most fears.

Strategy #3. "Perception" and "expectations" are more important than what we offer.

For example, we could offer an excellent business opportunity. But what if our prospects perceive the opportunity as something that is too hard to do? Or, what if our prospects expect everyone to say "yes," and then they get rejected?

These issues are much more important than some PowerPoint presentation. And this is what separates the professionals from the amateurs.

Here is an example.

If we give our new team members the expectation that only some people will say "yes," they won't be destroyed when someone turns them down. It will be expected.

How do we do this?

Tell our new team members that almost everyone needs our product or opportunity. However, today may not be the best time for them to take advantage of it. Why?

- They are busy at the exact time we call.
- We don't know what happened to them 30 minutes before we contacted them.
- They could have lost their jobs and are busy with that issue.
- They are recovering from a previous visit by a sleazy salesman.
- They had an argument with their spouse and can't think about anything else right now.

There could be other reasons, but we get the idea.

Our obligation is to give them the opportunity. We are not obligated to make decisions for other people. We don't want to be responsible for their lives. Plus, if we withhold our offer from them, that would mean we are making the decision for them. That is unfair. That is why we present our offer as an option.

Strategy #4. Remind our prospects that this is something we do FOR people, not TO people.

Our intention should be to give people one more option for their lives. Then, allow them to choose that option if the timing is right.

If our intention is to sell someone something so we can qualify for a commission or rank advancement, that will show in our micro-facial expressions, our body language, our tone of voice, and our words. Prospects are smart. They can sense our intentions.

When we have good intentions, not only do we remove our fear, but we will get better reactions from our prospects.

WHY GRASSHOPPERS CAN'T DRIVE.

Here is why grasshoppers can't drive.

Take one grasshopper and put him in the driver's seat of your car.

Then yell, "Drive!"

What does the grasshopper do? Nothing.

And this proves that grasshoppers:

- Are lazy.
- Have no motivation.
- Can't hear.
- Lost their vision board.
- Don't "want it" bad enough.
- Didn't have a strong enough "why."
- Flunked out of personal development school.
- Have loser attitudes.
- Are uncoachable.

These would be the **wrong** conclusions.

We never taught the grasshopper **how** to drive. So how could we possibly expect the grasshopper to know how to drive? (Okay, and their legs are too short.)

It is the same with us and our team members. We didn't learn the step-by-step "how to" for motivation, talking to prospects, or presenting. They didn't teach that at my school. What about yours?

We tell our team members, "Get motivated! Take action now!"

How does that work out?

Usually, not well.

Then we shout:

- "Face the fear, and the fear will go away." (Haven't seen much of that happening.)
- "Every 'no' gets us closer to another 'yes.'" (The reality? It gets us closer to another 'no,' so we don't even try.
- "Victory goes to those that take action!" (Sounds good, but it's hard to get started.)
- "Just talk to more people!" (And our team will repeat the words that didn't work last time.)

So when our team isn't moving forward, we jump to the wrong conclusion. We assume they are lazy and unmotivated.

But think about our new team members. They gave up a night of television to come to our presentation. They reached into their pocket and invested their hard-earned money. Does this sound like they are lazy and unmotivated?

Of course not.

They want to work. They want to succeed. But they just don't know exactly what to do.

They talk to people, say the wrong things, and get rejected. It won't take them long to pick up the trend. And then they stop.

Ready for a solution?

THE TEST NETWORK MARKETERS ARE AFRAID TO TAKE.

A dog chases a car. The dog never thinks, "What will I do if I catch the car?"

The good news is our new team members can't wait to talk to prospects. "This opportunity is amazing! I want to tell everyone right now."

We love it when positive mindsets drive people to successful activities. But as smart sponsors, we can do more.

Because here is the bad news. When our new, untrained team finally gets prospects to listen to them, they don't know what to say!

When we join, we see the big picture of our business. We understand what this business can mean for us. Exciting times! We naturally assume that everyone will have our same clear vision. And, that is not true.

Many prospects have life experiences and programs that hold them back. They are skeptical. They look for reasons not to change. And they don't believe that anything good can happen for them. These are our future negative prospects.

Our new team member will meet these people shortly. We can pre-arm them with a few sentences and skills now. Why not give them the best chance of success when they talk to their first prospects?

An easy way to explain this is to imagine that prospecting will require two basic skills.

Skill #1: Locating prospects to talk to. If we don't have anyone to talk to, nothing will happen.

Skill #2: Saying the right words to our prospects. If our prospects don't believe or trust us, they will never join.

When I started network marketing, I talked to hundreds of prospects. No results. These prospects were not dumb. They wanted an opportunity. Unfortunately, they didn't like how I **described** the opportunity. Even if they wanted the opportunity desperately, when I opened my mouth, they changed their minds.

New team members have prospects to talk to. We should coach them on the words to say. If our new team members balk at learning what to say, we can give them this little test. This should convince them that they need to invest a few moments in training before approaching their prospects. While we may want to accompany them on their first appointments, it may not always be possible.

Ready? Here is the little five-question test.

Question #1: What is your best ice breaker sentence? Write it down now, word-for-word.

Question #2: What is your best "sound bite" for your products or services? Write it down now, word-for-word.

Question #3: What is your best one- or two-sentence closing statement? Write it down now, word-for-word.

Question #4: What is your best belief and trust sentence to build rapport with your prospect? Write it down now, word-for-word.

Question #5: What is your best one-sentence answer to the question, "What do you do for a living?" Write it down now, word-for-word.

Before going further, let's take this test ourselves right now.

Have you written down your answers to these five questions? Choose which of the following statements applies to you.

- I did not have answers. Maybe this is why network marketing is difficult for me.
- I did not have answers. I will send my new team members to talk to others, totally untrained. This will not end well.
- I was too lazy to write down the answers. No comment.
- I pretended to know the answers. Hoping and wishing is my current strategy.
- I have clear, word-for-word answers to these five questions. I can help my new team members.

Regardless of how we personally score here, we have to get serious right now if we are to serve our new team members. So, back to them.

Of course our new team members don't have answers to these questions.

We will get a blank sheet of paper, or some cringe-worthy scribbling.

Our team members now have open minds. They will pay attention to our suggested answers. When they know these answers, their confidence levels will go up. Prospects react positively to confident presenters. It will now be easier for them to enroll new members.

Want some examples of sample answers? Here are some to start with, but we should have our favorites already.

Question #1: What is your best ice breaker sentence?

- "I just found out how we can work out of our homes instead of fighting traffic to a job."
- "I am just curious, would you like to lose weight just by changing what you have for breakfast?"
- "Do you like taking good care of your skin?"
- "What would you do with the money from an extra paycheck every month?"
- "Do you hate how much vacations cost?"
- "Do you find that growing old really hurts?"
- "Are you okay with working 45 years like our parents?"

Question #2: What is your best "sound bite" for your products or services?

- "This turns our bodies into fat-burning machines."
- "Make money every time our friends pick up their phones."
- "Two paychecks are better than one."
- "Our face is our best first impression."
- "Wrinkles are overrated."
- "Feel like you are 16 years old again, but with better judgment."
- "Take a five-star holiday for the price of a Holiday Inn."

Question #3: What is your best one- or two-sentence closing statement?

- "This either works for you, or not. So what do you want to do?"

- "What is going to be easier for you? To continue getting by on one paycheck, or to start building your extra paycheck tonight?"

- "Does it make sense to get started now, instead of trying to get by on one paycheck?"

- "Would it be okay to get started now, so we could do this together?"

- "So, now it is your choice. To start a business now, or to put it off for later."

Question #4: What is your best belief and trust sentence to build rapport with your prospect?

- "Most people feel that jobs take up too much time during our week."

- "Well, you know how we don't have time to exercise to lose weight?"

- "Do you hate this job is much as I do?"

- "Well, you know how vacations and holidays are so expensive?"

- "Do you ever notice how things are more expensive now?"

- "Ever notice how wrinkles multiply as we get older?"

- "Do you hate fighting traffic to work as much as I do?"

Question #5: What is your best one-sentence answer to the question, "What do you do for a living?"

- "I show people how to make their skin younger while they sleep."
- "I help people work out of their homes, so they don't have to commute to work."
- "I show moms how to stay home with their children, so they don't have to warehouse them in daycare while they work a full-time job."
- "I help people lose weight one time, and keep it off forever."
- "I show people how to fire their boss and have their own business."

When new team members start, they will naturally go to their best prospects first. So let's arm them with some good sentences. They should have good rapport with these new prospects. This is their golden opportunity to get off to a faster start.

Why is this five-question test so important?

Because it is what we do **before** we come into contact with our prospects that will make the most difference.

Think about professional athletes. What do they do for years and years before they participate as professionals? They learn the skills and they practice. They don't show up at the sporting event one day and say, "Let me just wing it. Let's see what I can do."

Every professional tennis player, football player, or boxer learned what to do, and then practiced before the competition.

Their coach didn't say, "Just go out and get 100 defeats. Every defeat gets you closer to a win."

So, we shouldn't say, "Just go out and get 100 'no' answers and rejections. Every 'no' gets you closer to a 'yes.'"

That wouldn't even be true. Why?

Because if we are saying the wrong words that consistently get us "no" answers, then every "no" answer gets us closer to the next "no" answer. This will not fix itself.

Answering these five questions should at least be the minimum beginning lesson for our new team members.

RESISTANCE.

It only takes one excuse to stop new team members from working.

One.

In the beginning, new team members have many concerns and objections. The most serious concerns could stop them from moving forward. Our strategy is to have satisfying answers for their most pressing fears. This modified story from *Mini-Scripts for the Four Color Personalities* illustrates how doubt can hold us back.

***

We want to buy a bigger home. The agent takes us to a beautiful neighborhood, and shows us the perfect home. Enough bedrooms? Yes. Enough bathrooms? Yes. Are the neighborhood schools great? Yes. The neighbors? The friendliest people we've ever met.

Everything is perfect except one little thing. When we look out of the back window of our potential dream home, we notice a large dam. In one corner of the dam there are small cracks. We ask the agent, "Does this dam hold a lot of water?" The agent replies, "Yes. It holds the water for the entire city."

We then ask the agent, "Do you see those small cracks over in the corner of the dam?" He replies, "Yes. Those cracks have been there a long time. Don't worry about them."

Later we return home to think about the house we saw. What do we think about the most?

Yes, the cracks in the dam. We worry that if we buy this home, we will make a huge mistake. Everything else is perfect. But even though the agent assured us that those small cracks were nothing unusual, we continue to worry about those cracks in the dam.

What happens? We eventually look for a different home to buy. We give up on our dream home and buy a home that is inferior, but we feel safe that we did not make a bad decision.

***

We can show new team members the most incredible opportunity in the world. But a single, tiny flaw can hold their attention and prevent them from moving forward.

So when is a good time to discuss these paralyzing problems?

Before they surface, of course.

If we wait until after the paralyzing problems appear, dealing with them will be much harder. Either way, we must be prepared to explain how these problems won't be career-killers.

Humans fear making mistakes. This fear comes from our survival programs. The fear is real, but fear does not mean we can't still go ahead. If our answers to their fears are satisfactory, that will be the first step to move our new team members over their obstacles.

If our answers to their fears are unsatisfactory, team members default to this strategy:

Sitting on the sidelines, hoping something will happen in their business. Ouch.

Let's look at some common fears and problems our new team members will face.

"THEY DON'T WANT MY HELP!"

We can't be mentors if our new team members can't be coached.

Many new team members have their own ideas on how they want to do network marketing. They will ignore our advice and try to do it their way.

Why? Maybe they have a special skill that is hard to duplicate, and they want to apply it to their business. Or maybe they have a special source of prospects.

Or, they could be natural-born leaders and self-starters, and they don't want to hear our advice. They already know how to do everything better than anyone else.

Before we discourage them, let's consider this. They are self-starters. That is good. We love self-starters.

Here is a tactful way to offer them some guidance. Simply say:

"About 15 million other distributors started out on the same journey you are about to take. Would you like to know some interesting secrets they discovered?"

Most will say, "Yes."

It is a lot easier to offer advice when it is requested. We honor their opinion that they know the best way to do it. We don't attack their ego by saying, "Listen to me." Instead, we pass on some secrets that they would like to know.

And what could we pass on first?

How about the five-question test we just finished?

Now, will this be a problem for our new team members?

When they sponsor their first team members, will their new team want to listen to their advice?

Ah, they will experience this too. But now we have prepared them for this problem. They will know to say:

"About 15 million other distributors started out on the same journey you are about to take. Would you like to know some interesting secrets they discovered?"

Does this "do-it-myself" belief apply to everyone?

No. Most team members want help and advice from their sponsors. They look forward to communicating with us regularly.

Do we have a system to keep in touch with our team? If not, network marketing professional Holly Martin has this great seven-day rule. She says, "Talk to each team member at least once every seven days, and more often early in their careers."

We are sponsors. That means new team members should not have to figure this out alone.

HELPING NEW TEAM MEMBERS WITH REJECTION.

"No."

"No."

"No."

"No."

Four rejections in a row! I couldn't believe it.

It was a late, rainy Sunday evening. Art Jonak, his daughter Julie, and I were leaving a night market in Thailand.

I rushed out into the rain to see if the first taxi driver in line would take us where we needed to go. "No." That was a short reply. The second taxi driver at least paused before announcing, "No."

I was getting soaked in the rain. Art and Julie were staying dry under a roof in the market.

Taxi driver #3 and taxi driver #4 didn't want to take us where we wanted to go.

And now, the decision.

1. Should I try to convince the first four taxi drivers to change their minds, abandon their objections, and schedule a follow-up? Or,

2. Should I ask taxi driver #5 for a ride?

The rain water was already running down the back of my pants, so I opted for choice #2. I asked the driver of taxi #5 if he would take us to where we wanted to go.

It turned out that taxi driver #5 was more than happy to take the three of us to where we wanted to go. He didn't even mind the wet spot I left on the back seat covers.

When we are in a hurry, rejection doesn't seem to bother us much. We get on with doing what we have to do to get the job done. We needed a ride.

So if we hate rejection, one way of dealing with our feelings is to be in a hurry. Then, we don't have time to feel bad for ourselves.

Try this thought process the next time we get rejected. Ask ourselves this question:

1. "Should I invest the next few minutes, hours, or weeks trying to convince my prospect to change his mind?" Or,

2. "Would it be easier simply to spend less than 10 seconds asking someone else if they are interested?"

Choice #2 looks pretty good now.

We don't have professional psychologist qualifications. Some prospects might even take years to convince. Maybe this is something we can do **after** we build our network marketing business. When we are rich and retired, we can volunteer our time for these hard-core cases.

But while building our business? It makes more sense to spend 10 seconds asking someone else if they are interested.

We are in a hurry to reach our initial goals. It might be a huge part-time income, or even a full-time income. We want to leave the pain and frustration of our current circumstances behind, and move forward quickly. Just like I got tired of having rain pouring down the back of my pants and wanted to get inside a dry taxi.

When we present prospecting in this way to our new team members, they won't take rejection personally. They simply see it as a signal to ask someone else. Now they will be spending more productive time talking to prospects with immediate potential, instead of nurturing the same handful of prospects for months and years.

What could hold our team members back from this viewpoint?

They could think, "But I don't have more people to talk to. Let me nurture these people who told me 'no.' That way I don't have to go out and meet new people."

This is why we have to have a rejection-free first sentence for our team members. They need a tool to create a constant supply of new prospects. Once they feel that they have unlimited future prospects to talk to, they won't cling to their current non-prospects.

I DON'T WANT TO BOTHER MY FRIENDS AND FAMILY.

Imagine we had a cure for cancer. Would we let others know about it? Yes!

It would be up to them to decide whether or not to take the cure. But we would at least want them to know that a cure was available.

What if they didn't believe in the cure? No problem. Again, we would want them to know. It would be immoral of us to decide to keep the cure top secret. We would always want to think, "At least I let them know about the cure. It was their choice to take the cure or not."

We should have the same feeling about our network marketing message. We want our friends and family to know about our products, services, and business. If they choose to buy or participate, that is their choice. If they choose not to buy or participate, that is their choice also. Leaving them with a choice means less rejection. Plus we will never feel bad about withholding our benefits from them.

If we can instill this belief into our new team members, they won't be afraid to talk to others. Instead, they can give the option to others without stress. Most stress is self-induced. It comes from creating imaginary stories in our minds.

What are some phrases we can teach our new team members so that they can introduce their business comfortably? Here are a few.

"This may or may not be your cup of tea. But I at least wanted you to know what I am doing. I started a new part-time business, and wanted to know if you would like to hear the details."

That wasn't too scary. We announced that it may or may not be for them, so they already have an excuse not to hear what we have to say. This should help them relax. Then, we also asked them if they wanted to hear more details or not. That is polite.

Very few relatives and friends would be rude in their responses. And if someone was rude, we make a mental note that they may be a negative force that could contaminate the rest of our group. It is best to leave them out of our group.

"I got tired of trying to get by on my limited salary. So, I started a part-time business to help me get by. Would you like to hear more?"

We give the reason why we chose our part-time business. Then, we gave them the option of requesting more details if they are interested. It would be easy for them to say "no" to our question. No pressure on them. We should be just fine. They don't even have to prejudge our business, come up with reasons why it won't work, etc. All they have to say is "no" to more details.

"I finally found some skincare that worked on my daughter's acne. Do you know anyone with kids who struggle with acne?"

No pressure on the person we are talking to. We didn't ask them to buy, or even look at our product. So how does this look from the other person's standpoint? She might be thinking,

"You are trying to help people. Great. I will see if there is anyone I know that could use your help."

"I lowered my electricity bill by $20 a month. And I helped my mom lower her bill by $15 a month. Would you like me to lower your electricity bill also?"

In this case, we gave the benefits first. While everyone wants to lower their bills, some people are afraid of change and an unknown future. We want to make change less scary for them. In this case we might say, "It only took 10 minutes to lower my mom's bills."

"You hate dieting even more than I do. Would you like to know what I eat every morning at breakfast that keeps me so slim?"

If this sounds interesting to our prospects, they will ask, "What do you eat for breakfast?" If they don't ask us what we eat for breakfast, no problem. We can continue eating our breakfast and losing weight, while they continue gaining weight.

"Uncle, you are going to be retiring soon. I know at least one more way to add to your pension. Let me know when you would like to chat about it."

That sounds pretty safe. In fact, it sounds much better than, "When can I give you my complete 45-minute business presentation?" If our uncle is not interested now, guess what? Once our uncle does decide that more income would be better, he will remember us, and remember us fondly. We were not pushy. Instead, we showed respect. This would help us get off to a good start.

"I started a part-time business with a discount travel agency. Now you and I can take our holidays at wholesale prices instead of retail prices. How does that sound to you?"

Our brother-in-law might think, "Well, paying less for our family holiday makes a lot of sense. And, if you are doing it too, it must be a great way to save. I will have you as my trusted friend to sort out the best deals for me." Chances are that our brother-in-law will reply, "Tell me more." We can take it from there.

"My oversized shirts started feeling tight. I had to lose weight quickly. Do you know anyone who needs to shed ten pounds quickly?"

A little humor never hurts. Prospects smile. That is a good start. And, we could get a great referral. Just be careful not to say this to an overweight relative or friend.

Not only do these sentences make it safe for us to talk to family and friends, but we can also use these sentences with strangers.

Now there is no excuse not to talk to new people.

REPUTATION MOTIVATION.

Humans worry about what others think of them. This is part of our DNA from thousands of years of tribal programming. To get kicked out of the tribe meant trying to survive alone. That usually ended in death.

I know we hear, "Don't worry about what others think." But we do! It is a natural concern.

Our reputations are important to us. And for our new team members, one of the first things they worry about is what others will think. They worry:

- "Will others think I joined a pyramid scheme?"
- "Will others think I am just a salesperson, only concerned about making commissions from them?"
- "Will others laugh behind my back and secretly hope for me to fail?"
- "Will others think that I am not committed and will jump to the next shiny object?"
- "Will others think I am guaranteed to fail?"

These thoughts can paralyze our new team members.

Our strategy?

To divert the new team members' focus to a public commitment. We want new team members to publicly announce to their friends and family that not only have they joined a new business, but they are committed to making it work.

Now, it is much harder to back out of the commitment when we've made it public. Think about dieting. If no one knows we are dieting, it is easy to quit. If everyone knows we are dieting, and we told them that we are going to succeed, it is much harder to quit.

The longer our new team members work, the better their odds of eventual success in their business.

Why? Over time we gain more experience and better skills.

What kind of an announcement can new team members make? Well, let's imagine that we started today. What would we say to our friends and relatives?

- "I thought I would give this a try."
- "Testing this seems like a good idea to see if it works or not."
- "I am trying this for two weeks. If I don't see any progress, I will quit."
- "Oh, I am just checking this out."

These kinds of statements won't get anyone to join our team. No one wants to follow someone who is not committed. They don't want to die with us on our journey.

Now, what if we said this instead:

- "This is the business for me."
- "I gave my future some thought, and this is what I want to do."
- "I am going all the way to the top on this. It would be fun if you joined me on this journey."
- "It may take me a while to learn this business, but I am committed."

- "I needed a new career. I researched my options, and I will do this."

Our friends and relatives will have a different feeling about our commitment. When they detect our sincerity, it is easier for them to commit to joining us.

But the real value is what this commitment does to us and our new team members. We publicly stated what we are going to do. With this public commitment, people will look at what we do as an important part of our reputation. Now we are less likely to quit. Everyone has pride in their reputation.

Where and how can we make this announcement? Here are some ideas.

In the "notification principle" skill, one way of announcing our new business is to send a postcard, email, or text message to our family and friends. This is similar to opening a shoe store. We want to announce that we have a business. We don't have to plead with our family and friends to come to our shoe store. But, if they need shoes in the future, we would hope they would think of us. We can make that same type of announcement for our new network marketing business.

Social media? That is an inexpensive way to let others know about our commitment to our new business. We don't even have to pay for postage.

In-person social events? Everyone asks, "What is new with you?" Now we can share our commitment to our new business.

Even the simple act of ordering business cards makes our commitment look more real.

As leaders, let's ask ourselves this question: "Will my team members be more committed after a public announcement?" Of course the answer is, "Yes."

When new team members have their reputations attached to their business opportunity, they take it more seriously. They are less likely to quit. And we know our business will be on their minds several times a day.

HOW TO GET TEAM MEMBERS TO EVENTS AND TRAININGS.

Some team members start shrinking their business immediately after starting. Why?

They don't know what they don't know.

We know that we either grow or shrink each day. Our personal development doesn't stand still.

Yet, many new team members insist on avoiding their sponsor's training, refuse to read books, won't attend events, and generally stop their learning and growing. That is a shame.

So here is a fun question that we can ask our team members to get them to come to attend events and trainings.

"Do you want to come to our next training session, or are you happy to have your business peak at the current level?"

This question immediately points out the value of attending.

We can also use this question for upcoming big events. At events, many things happen.

- Social proof. We see that others made the same decision we did to be with this company.
- Relate to someone successful. Maybe a speaker is a truck driver, and we are truck drivers. Now we can visualize that we could have the same success.

- One new idea from the event could change our careers forever. We have to learn new ideas. They seldom come automatically in our sleep.

So the next time a team member is reluctant to attend a training or event, ask them: "Do you want to come to our next event, or are you happy to have your business peak at the current level?"

This question offers an option. The choice is:

1. Keep my business the same. Don't grow or earn more.

2. Come to the training or the event.

Humans love easy, simple choices.

One more example.

If our new team member resists attending our Saturday training, we could say this.

"Did we ever walk away from a conversation thinking, 'Oh my. I wish I would have said this.' Happens all the time. We think of the perfect answer after the conversation is over.

"The same thing happens in network marketing. We meet a great prospect. The conversation goes well, but not well enough to get an appointment. We walk away thinking to ourselves, 'I wonder what I could have said to get a better result?'

"Here is the question. When is the best time to learn exactly what to say to prospects? Before we meet them? Or after we meet them?"

The answer is obvious. Our new team member says, "Before we meet them."

Our reply? "That is why we're having our training this Saturday. I will send you the training video link now."

BUT A STRANGER TOLD ME, "NOBODY MAKES ANY MONEY!"

Ouch. Sometimes we have to play the psychologist. Our new team members can easily get their feelings hurt early in their careers. Because they are unsure, they are hyper-sensitive to criticism from others. Strangers will want to dump negative thoughts into their minds.

Without a strong belief in the business, there will be struggles. Prospects can read in our faces, in the tone of our voices, and in our words how much we believe in our business. Technical scripts and skills won't fix this. The core belief in the business must be there. This is why we will take extra time to instill belief in our team members.

Here is the scenario.

Team members approach us with tears in their eyes, a refund request in their hands, and say, "We want to quit. A stranger told us that nobody makes money in network marketing. Everybody loses money. Only people at the top earn money, but everyone else loses big money. People work for months, or even years, and never get paid. We don't know how to answer this objection, so we better resign now and give up on our dreams."

This is easy to fix, once we know how. We will use stories and analogies. Then, we deliver our message in a way that they will remember.

Let's start by investigating why a stranger would dump this negativity on other people's dreams.

This stranger had a bad experience. As humans, we make many of our judgments based upon past experiences. Here is an example.

You and I go to a restaurant. Your meal was excellent, a total 5-star experience. My meal was garbage. Undercooked, bad flavor, and the waiter coughed on my meal when he brought it from the kitchen. I didn't like my meal at all.

We both post restaurant reviews on the Internet. Your review said, "This is the best restaurant ever! My mouth waters every time I think of my last meal there. I even dream about that meal."

My review of the restaurant? "Never go to this restaurant! Avoid this restaurant. Evil demons work in the kitchen and the waiters are vampires. Stay away!"

Now it is obvious what happened to our negative stranger. He had a bad experience. And this is his review of his bad experience: "Everybody loses money. Only people at the top earn money, but everyone else loses big money. People work for months, or even years, and never get paid."

For our negative stranger, this is a legitimate review. We should honor this. No need to argue with the negative stranger. But this isn't the whole story. We will get to the whole story in a moment. For now, let's concern ourselves with our shaken team members who are hearing the negative review.

Let's have a meal with them. We are going to use stories and analogies to re-instill belief in our business.

The NBA story.

450 million people in the world play basketball.

Almost everyone who plays basketball loses money.

They spend money on expensive and endorsed basketball shoes. Hundreds of dollars wasted. Years of their lives wasted practicing their crossover dribble. Transportation to and from practices costs money. Many people go to basketball camps that have high tuition fees. Some even pay for personal coaches. What a money-losing proposition!

Out of the 450 million people who play basketball, how many are at the top earning big money in the NBA? Only a few people at the top earn money, but everyone else loses big money. People play basketball for months, or even years, and never get paid!

A few lucky people could earn a college scholarship, or even play for a minor league team and earn some money. But everyone else? They will lose money.

Does this mean that no one should play basketball?

Of course not. What are some of the things people get when they play basketball?

- Exercise. It is great for their health.
- They learn the value of teamwork.
- They create new friends.
- They build a network.
- They avoid becoming a "couch potato."
- They enjoy some friendly competition.
- They have fun playing the game with friends.
- They experience the value of practicing skills.

Is playing in the NBA within our control?

No.

Here is the downside. We could invest money and practice endlessly. But, we are subject to the whims of the people who choose players for their 17-player team roster.

Yes, only a tiny percentage of people will ever play for a NBA team and earn big money. The rest of us? We will have to settle for the other benefits of playing basketball.

To summarize:

- The NBA only pays a few people at the top.
- There are still good reasons to play basketball.
- We can't control if we are chosen in the NBA annual draft, or if we qualify for the team.

I want to be a movie star.

How many people take drama classes in high school? Or at university? So many people want to be an actor or actress. The few people at the very top can earn millions of dollars by starring in a movie.

They study hard, invest in classes, and do free performances throughout the year. No one gets paid. Everyone loses money paying for acting classes and coaches. People drive to endless auditions only to be overlooked. And professional photos are not cheap.

And if we do make it to Hollywood? The chances of even becoming an extra on a movie set are slim.

Everywhere we drive we meet unemployed actors and actresses in part-time jobs or full-time jobs, while they are hoping to break into the business. Millions and millions of people want to be famous movie stars, but the math doesn't lie. Only a select few will earn the big money. The rest? They hope for gasoline reimbursement to drive back and forth to their free performances.

Does this mean that no one should become an actor or actress? Of course not. What are some of the things people get from performing?

- Recognition. On the stage, they are stars.
- A chance to express their creative selves.
- Competition. They won the role over others.
- And they develop a community of friends who love the arts.

Is becoming a movie star within our control?

No.

Here is the downside. We could invest money, practice for decades, but we are subject to the whims of directors who pick actors and actresses for movies. Auditions are mass rejection. And even if we got picked to be in a movie, would it be for the starring role? Probably not. The odds are astronomically against us.

To summarize:

- Only a few people become highly-paid movie stars.
- There are still good reasons to enjoy acting.
- Auditions are not within our control. Our future depends on others.

The "start my own business" story.

We've heard this hundreds of times: "9 out of 10 businesses fail in the first few years."

There is some truth in this. Why do these businesses fail?

- Former employees who are trying their own businesses for the first time.
- Lack of capital.
- Great skills, but no knowledge of how business works.
- The local economy goes bad.
- A bigger company takes their customers.
- Advertising costs a lot.

Yes, there are many ways a new business can fail. The entire investment is lost. There is no guarantee.

But does that mean no one should start a business? What would our world look like if no one started businesses? Pretty sad.

Many business people work hard, and may never earn a profit. For the surviving businesses? Some will give the owner a part-time income or help support the family.

Is becoming a successful business owner within our control?

Nothing in life is entirely within our control, but our odds are vastly better!

We can control how hard we work. We can control how many skills we decide to learn. And, we don't have a coach or audition director with total control over our career.

Are there advantages to starting our own business? Yes.

- We learn new life skills.
- We have a chance to be our own boss.
- We expand our network of contacts and friends.
- We choose our own hours.
- We have an opportunity to earn more than a salary.
- We can offer a product or service that helps others.

Yes, when people start a new business, we see smiles on their faces.

To summarize:

- Only a few business people ultimately become millionaires or billionaires.
- We feel happy when we work for ourselves.
- With the new skills we learn, we become better people.
- We have more control over our ultimate success than we would if we were actors or NBA players.

The network marketing story.

How many people want to start their own business, but don't want to take a huge risk?

We hear about superstar network marketers making huge amounts monthly. Of course, these people are the exceptions. For us, we might feel happy with a few hundred dollars extra a month.

- We don't have an opportunity to earn extra money in our full-time jobs.
- We don't have extra money to invest in a business.

- We don't want to risk our family's security by investing large amounts of cash and debt into a business franchise.
- We can't afford to quit our jobs to start a new business.
- We don't want the burden of long leases, overhead, and staffing of a business.

Is there still an opportunity for us?

Yes. We call it "network marketing."

In network marketing we can invest our time and effort, with very little cash expenditure, to create customers and team members for our business.

Will we need new skills for this profession? Yes. But we can invest and learn. We spend money on products and services, transportation costs to rallies and trainings, and sometimes a babysitter, if needed. There will be a cost.

Does that mean everyone will become a successful superstar in network marketing?

No. Not at all.

For most people, the time and skill-learning commitment won't fit their lives' goals. They may be impatient. Or, they have other more important goals in their lives.

Does this mean that no one should get involved in network marketing? Of course not. What are a few of the benefits people receive from their network marketing part-time business?

- Personal development. For me, I had never heard the word "goals" until I joined network marketing.
- New friends. Positive people that enhance our social lives.
- A great product or service experience.
- An opportunity to help and serve others.

- A possible part-time bonus check to help with our monthly budget.
- A chance to have hope in our lives that we did not have before.

Is becoming a network marketing superstar within our control?

No.

But, our odds will be better than becoming a movie star or NBA player for sure!

The good news is that we have some control over our future. We don't have a "gatekeeper" that tells us, "You are chosen." Or, "You are not chosen."

We can increase our odds of success by learning new skills, and by working more effectively. This is great news. We feel motivated when we know our efforts make a difference.

Yes, a few people will become superstars in network marketing. Many more will earn full-time incomes. And many, many more will earn part-time incomes. And there will be a huge number of network marketers who enjoy the benefits of the products, or the new connections in their lives.

To summarize:

- Only a few people will become network marketing superstars.
- Many will earn an income.
- Many more will enjoy the other benefits of network marketing.
- We have more control over our ultimate success.

Now, about that negative critic that said, "Nobody makes any money!" Why is this critic so negative about network marketing? This person had a bad experience in network marketing, or had a friend with a bad experience. They joined to become a network marketing superstar, and it didn't happen. And, they didn't get a good part-time income either.

Based on their experience, they will leave a negative review. And that is something interesting about people. We love sharing bad news.

Not everyone will get what they want in life. But that should not mean that we give up trying. For many, network marketing is our chance to change our lives.

So when we become successful in network marketing, realize that some people did not. And for them, their anti-network marketing opinions are valid.

WHEN PROBLEMS AND CHALLENGES HIT THEM HEAD-ON.

Problems never go away. No matter how successful we become, problems will continue.

For our new team members, we train them how to face their problems when we are not there. We can't hold their hands forever. We can't send them out prospecting covered in bubble-wrap.

The other option is to train new team members to avoid problems. But, that is impossible to do. Problems lurk everywhere. We call this life.

Yes, we could step in and fix their problems. That would be quick and efficient. However, we will have to step in and fix the next problem. And the next problem. Instead of us fixing or telling them how to solve the problems, we should teach them how to solve the problems on their own. Here is our chance to empower our team.

Let's give them a guideline to follow. In this case, we will give them three questions to remember.

Question #1: "What is the challenge or goal that is holding us back now?"

They might say, "I can't see myself talking to cold prospects." Or, "The qualifications for the company trip are too high for me to achieve."

We don't want our conversations to go in a thousand different directions. We must be clear about what the real problem is. This will keep our discussion focused solely on the problem at hand.

Question #2: "What skill or ability do you feel you are missing to solve this challenge?"

Their reply? "I don't know how to find new people." Or, "I can't communicate with people that refuse to listen."

Now we have the problem, and the real reason that holds them back. They point out exactly what they will have to learn to fix this problem. Problems are easier to deal with when we understand them and their solutions.

It is the unknown that gives us stress.

Question #3: "What do you think you should do next? Learn a new skill? Find another way of solving this challenge?"

For example, imagine they don't know how to find new prospects. They could learn better skills for local prospecting. However, maybe they are uncomfortable with that. So, what else could they do?

They could learn social media skills. They could purchase some advertising. They could make connections with influencers who could send them pre-sold prospects. Yes, sometimes they may not have the ability or the desire to learn a new skill. In that case, let's be creative.

Challenges and problems happen. We won't let them hold our team members back. We will ask them these three questions to keep their careers moving forward.

When to implement this.

Immediately!

From the time new team members join, instead of giving them quick answers, we can take them through this three-step process.

After going through this process many times, our new team members won't fear problems. They will see problems as part of the business. Now, when they are on their own, they have a template to follow.

Network marketing leader Simon Chan has a great quote that I love:

"There are two primary choices in life:

"1. You can accept conditions as they exist, or

"2. Accept the responsibility for changing the conditions."

Sounds harsh, doesn't it?

But, sometimes we have to face the hard truth.

Now, as smart sponsors, we won't repeat this quote to someone who doesn't have the tools to fix their situation. That is where we come in. We are the experienced sponsors that know how to change the conditions. We will show our new team members the activities that can change their conditions.

Stupidity needs empathy.

Will new team members make stupid mistakes?

Of course. Guaranteed.

What should our reactions be?

Our emotional brains will have a harsh first impression.

Don't worry. This is natural. It is easy for us to label a team member as lazy or as a complainer the first time we hear negativity or see a stupid mistake. That is our brain activating its automatic judgment. We don't have much control over this part of our brain.

But, we can set our initial reactions aside. Instead of accepting the first impression, we can use the magic of empathy.

Empathy means we crawl into other people's minds, think of their past experiences, and try to feel what they are feeling.

People who disagree with us are not dumb. As humans, we make the best decisions we can based upon our beliefs, programs, and the information we have at hand.

So, how do others come to their crazy conclusions? Why do they disagree with us? Why do they not believe us? Why do they act the way they do?

Because they had different experiences in their lives. Our experiences help shape our decisions and our actions. For example, if a dog bites us when we are young, we may have an irrational fear of dogs forever.

People have programs in their lives. Programs are beliefs given to us from parents, teachers, and yes, even repeated stories on the news. Even big lies can become "truths" in our brains if repeated often enough. Some people call this "brainwashing."

People don't go out of their way to make stupid, idiotic decisions that make their lives worse.

Now, we may encounter resistance to our ideas or suggestions. Let's ask ourselves, "Why? What has this person experienced to cause this resistance?"

Then, we try to understand and have empathy. We might ask questions. Or, we allow others to explain their resistance to our ideas or suggestions. There are benefits here.

First, we now comprehend their viewpoints. They make more sense to us. We may still disagree, but we know which views we will have to change.

Second, when we understand others, they can feel it. We create a bond. Most relationships are superficial. But when we take the time and effort to understand others, this will create loyalty in our group. No one likes dictators who give orders without considering their viewpoints or the effects they have on other people.

WHAT MAKES US ATTRACTIVE AS SMART SPONSORS?

We only have to look at what **we** would want in a sponsor.

- Would we want a motivated or an unmotivated sponsor?
- Would we want a positive or a negative sponsor?
- Would we want a sponsor who is skilled or unskilled?
- Would we join a sponsor who made negative comments about others?
- Would we join a sponsor who complained about the company?
- Would we join a sponsor who tried to convince us that every company in our industry is bad except one?
- Would we join a sponsor who talked badly about other people?
- Would we want a sponsor who didn't have time for us?

It's easy to see why some sponsors do well and why some struggle.

But what stands out?

Prospects don't want a sponsor who criticizes and complains about others. Prospects see this sponsor as having low self-esteem and a low self-image.

How do we show this to new team members?

In our business, there are many people and things to criticize. We can't stick our heads in the sand and ignore negative situations. So how do we address them?

A mature way to look at this is, "Like most things, there is some good and bad." Here are some examples.

The company raises the prices of our products or services. Our response?

"Higher prices will mean we have to be better when we talk to prospects. On the plus side, higher prices will mean the company can make enough profit to stay in business. That is great for us."

Someone in our company does something unethical. How should we comment?

"That was unethical. People make mistakes and make poor judgments. On the plus side, this individual did make a decision to change his life by joining our business. I am sure his choices will be better in the future."

Taking the "high road" builds respect.

If we talk badly about others to our team, what would they think we say about them when they are not present?

We build respect by being respectful about others.

AND FINALLY.

We have a huge toolbox that makes our job easy. Here are a few of the tools we can use to help people step into the scary, unknown territory of a new career:

- Recognition and praise. Mary Kay Ash had it right. Generals know men will perform acts of courage for ribbons and medals. People crave recognition in their lives. There is an old saying, "People work for money, but they will die for recognition."

- Community. Humans want to belong. We are social by nature. We want acceptance in the group, and even more importantly, we want to feel comfortable in that group. When we help others join our community, they appreciate our efforts.

- Analogies. It is impossible for us to understand something well unless we can compare it to something we already know. Vague concepts are easily forgotten. They won't have any emotional impact or motivation in our lives. We will compare each new concept to something our new team members are familiar with.

- Stories. The human brain learns best with stories. That is our natural learning mode. We remember stories. We don't have to memorize facts.

- Expectations. People react to their expectations, not to events. We can choose to see most events from different viewpoints. We will create accurate expectations for both the good and bad things that will happen in our new team members' careers.

- Ability to perform. We will give our new team members activities they can do and enjoy. There is nothing more frustrating than the inability to do a desired task.

As smart sponsors, let's have the empathy and desire to help each new person on our team reach their true potential.

Thank you.

Thank you for purchasing and reading this book. We hope you found some ideas that will work for you.

Before you go, would it be okay if we asked a small favor? Would you take just one minute and leave a sentence or two reviewing this book online? Your review can help others choose what they will read next. It would be greatly appreciated by many fellow readers.

More Books from Big Al Books
BigAlBooks.com

Prospecting and Recruiting Series

How to Get Appointments Without Rejection
Fill Our Calendars with Network Marketing Prospects

Create Influence
10 Ways to Impress and Guide Others

How to Meet New People Guidebook
Overcome Fear and Connect Now

How to Get Your Prospect's Attention and Keep It!
Magic Phrases for Network Marketing

10 Shortcuts Into Our Prospects' Minds
Get network marketing decisions fast!

How To Prospect, Sell And Build Your Network Marketing Business With Stories

26 Instant Marketing Ideas To Build Your Network Marketing Business

51 Ways and Places to Sponsor New Distributors
Discover Hot Prospects For Your Network Marketing Business

First Sentences for Network Marketing
How To Quickly Get Prospects On Your Side

Big Al's MLM Sponsoring Magic
How To Build A Network Marketing Team Quickly

Start SuperNetworking!
5 Simple Steps to Creating Your Own Personal Networking Group

Getting Started Series

How to Build Your Network Marketing Business in 15 Minutes a Day

3 Easy Habits For Network Marketing
Automate Your MLM Success

Quick Start Guide for Network Marketing
Get Started FAST, Rejection-FREE!

Core Skills Series

How To Get Instant Trust, Belief, Influence and Rapport!
13 Ways To Create Open Minds By Talking To The Subconscious Mind

Ice Breakers!
How To Get Any Prospect To Beg You For A Presentation

Pre-Closing for Network Marketing
"Yes" Decisions Before The Presentation

The Two-Minute Story for Network Marketing
Create the Big-Picture Story That Sticks!

Personality Training Series (The Colors)

The Four Color Personalities for MLM
The Secret Language for Network Marketing

Mini-Scripts for the Four Color Personalities
How to Talk to our Network Marketing Prospects

Why Are My Goals Not Working?
Color Personalities for Network Marketing Success

How To Get Kids To Say Yes!
Using the Secret Four Color Languages to Get Kids to Listen

Presentation and Closing Series

Closing for Network Marketing
Getting Prospects Across The Finish Line

The One-Minute Presentation
Explain Your Network Marketing Business Like A Pro

How to Follow Up With Your Network Marketing Prospects
Turn Not Now Into Right Now!

Retail Sales for Network Marketers
How to Get New Customers for Your MLM Business

Leadership Series

The Complete Three-Book Network Marketing Leadership Series
Series includes: How To Build Network Marketing Leaders Volume One, How To Build Network Marketing Leaders Volume Two, and Motivation. Action. Results.

How To Build Network Marketing Leaders
Volume One: Step-By-Step Creation Of MLM Professionals

How To Build Network Marketing Leaders
Volume Two: Activities And Lessons For MLM Leaders

Motivation. Action. Results.
How Network Marketing Leaders Move Their Teams

More Books...

Why You Need to Start Network Marketing
How to Remove Risk and Have a Better Life

How To Build Your Network Marketing Nutrition Business Fast

How Speakers, Trainers, and Coaches Get More Bookings
12 Ways to Flood Our Calendars with Paid Events

How To Build Your Network Marketing Utilities Business Fast

Getting "Yes" Decisions
What insurance agents and financial advisors can say to clients

Public Speaking Magic
Success and Confidence in the First 20 Seconds

Worthless Sponsor Jokes
Network Marketing Humor

About the Authors

Keith Schreiter has 20+ years of experience in network marketing and MLM. He shows network marketers how to use simple systems to build a stable and growing business.

So, do you need more prospects? Do you need your prospects to commit instead of stalling? Want to know how to engage and keep your group active? If these are the types of skills you would like to master, you will enjoy his "how-to" style.

Keith speaks and trains in the U.S., Canada, and Europe.

Tom "Big Al" Schreiter has 40+ years of experience in network marketing and MLM. As the author of the original "Big Al" training books in the late '70s, he has continued to speak in over 80 countries on using the exact words and phrases to get prospects to open up their minds and say "YES."

His passion is marketing ideas, marketing campaigns, and how to speak to the subconscious mind in simplified, practical ways. He is always looking for case studies of incredible marketing campaigns that give usable lessons.

As the author of numerous audio trainings, Tom is a favorite speaker at company conventions and regional events.

Printed in Poland
by Amazon Fulfillment
Poland Sp. z o.o., Wrocław

66323802R00063